KU-287-656

Danes raiding a
Saxon homestead

KINGDOM OF GUTHRUM

Danish ships
sailing up
the Thames

Danes

Alfred built
a tower here

London   River Thames

KINGDOM OF KENT

Watchers on
the cliffs

Hastings
Hastinga the Dane
landed here

Danish ships looking for a place to land

Series 561

This book tells you something of what England was like a thousand years ago, and of the King, Alfred the Great, who was on the throne.

Helen Francis

KING ALFRED
the Great

by L. DU GARDE PEACH,
M.A., Ph.D., D.Litt.

with illustrations
by JOHN KENNEY

Publishers: Wills & Hepworth Ltd., Loughborough
First published 1956 © *Printed in England*

KING ALFRED THE GREAT

This book tells you something of what England was like a thousand years ago, and of the King, Alfred the Great, who was on the throne.

To-day England is one country, divided into counties like Yorkshire and Devonshire, but a thousand years ago it was made up of a number of small kingdoms, each with a different king. The Kingdom of Wessex, ruled by King Alfred, was the southern part of England. Further north there was the Kingdom of Mercia, and to the east, East Anglia. The five towns: Derby, Nottingham, Lincoln, Leicester and Stamford made up yet another kingdom, called The Five Boroughs.

If you look at the map at the end of this book, it will show you exactly how England was divided up.

Nearly all the people who dwelt in these little kingdoms lived in small towns and villages, working on the land, growing their own food, spinning and weaving the cloth for their clothes, and never going very far from their homes.

This was a simple way of living, and everybody could have been very happy, if it had not been for the Danes.

These were fierce sea-raiders from the North, who came in their long black ships and attacked the peaceful English farmers. No man's life was safe, and no one knew when he might return home from his work in the fields to find his wife and children gone, and his house burnt to the ground.

Into this troubled country, a little prince was born in Wessex. He was the son of Aethelwulf, the King, and Queen Osburga. His name was Alfred, and he grew up to be one of the wisest kings who ever sat on the English throne.

In those early days very few people could read or write, sometimes not even kings and queens. But Alfred's mother could read, and it was her example which encouraged Alfred to learn.

One day she was reading some stories to Alfred and his three brothers. The stories were not printed in a book, because printing had not yet been invented. Everything had to be written by hand and the pages of the manuscripts were decorated with gold and coloured letters.

Although Alfred could not read, he loved looking at the coloured pages, and wanted to have the book for his very own. Osburga saw how interested her sons were, and promised to give the book to the first of them who could read it. Alfred quickly found someone to teach him, and soon the book was his.

We know nothing about Alfred during the years when he was growing into a young man, but we do know that meanwhile the Danes were sending more and more men to invade England. Soon all the eastern and northern parts of the country were conquered by them.

Alfred's three elder brothers were all Kings of the English during this period and Alfred helped them to fight the Danes. But the first thing we know about him for certain is that he was married to Ealhswith when he was twenty years old, and it was a very splendid wedding in the Saxon Cathedral of Winchester.

Winchester Cathedral has been rebuilt since Alfred's marriage but there are still Saxon churches in England. We recognise them by the heavy undecorated pillars and round arches shown in the picture.

All this time there was fighting all over England between the Danes and the English, and usually the Danes had the better of it. However, in a battle at Ashdown, on the Berkshire Hills, when Alfred was only twenty-one, he and his soldiers won a great victory.

Near Uffington, where this battle was fought, there is the figure of a horse, cut in the turf on the hillside. Because the ground underneath is chalk the horse is white, and can clearly be seen to this day.

There is a tradition that this figure was cut by King Alfred's soldiers to celebrate the victory. This is probably only a story made up to account for it, because no-one can really be sure how old the white horse is.

The year after this battle, Alfred's third brother died, and Alfred became King over all Wessex.

In those days the King was not crowned in London, because it had been conquered by the Danes. So Alfred's coronation was in the old town of Winchester, the capital of Wessex, which was the south-western part of the country still held by the English.

Alfred rode on a horse to his coronation, surrounded by Saxons all armed and ready to fight the Danes at any moment. When he entered the Cathedral, the ceremony of the coronation was the same as when our present Queen Elizabeth was crowned, and as it has always been celebrated from that day to this.

If ever you go to Winchester, you should try to see the statue of King Alfred, standing proudly in the city in which he was crowned so long ago.

Alfred was now King, but he was not King of a peaceful, happy country, for the Danes were always attacking the towns and villages, and a great victory, like the one at Ashdown, was not repeated.

It was Christmastide, and like everyone else, King Alfred and his friends were enjoying a Christmas feast, at a place called Chippenham, in Wiltshire.

Then, suddenly, whilst they were all happily eating and drinking, there were shouts outside, and the sound of clashing swords. The Danes had come!

Alfred and his men seized their weapons and dashed out into the streets, leaving their Christmas dinner uneaten on the table. But they were so surprised and unprepared that their resistance was of no use, and the Danes, organized and fighting fiercely, were too strong for men who, only a moment before, had been thinking of nothing but enjoying a happy and peaceful Christmas.

Many of King Alfred's men were killed by the Danes, but he and a few faithful followers escaped and found refuge amongst the swamps and marshes at Athelney, in Somerset.

They crossed the swamps in little boats made of branches and the skins of animals, or on bundles of rushes tied together to form rafts, and built a camp on some firm ground in the middle. Here they thought they were safe.

But the Danes were soon hunting them again, determined to kill King Alfred and conquer England for themselves. Often Alfred and his soldiers had to hide, and disguise themselves, to escape their fierce enemies.

It was whilst Alfred was in hiding, disguised as a poor peasant, that he knocked one day at the door of a lonely hut in the marshes, and asked for shelter.

A peasant woman opened the door, and taking pity on Alfred, told him that he could come in and rest. She was baking some cakes, and asked Alfred to see that they did not burn, whilst she went to the well. But Alfred was thinking about how to beat the Danes, so he forgot all about the cakes, which were soon burnt to cinders.

When the woman returned and found her cakes ruined, she was naturally angry, and not knowing that Alfred was the King, she scolded him bitterly and even, as some of the stories tell, beat him with her broomstick.

We can well imagine the woman's sur-
prise when some of Alfred's followers
appeared and, going down on one knee,
saluted the ragged peasant as their King.
Quickly she too was on her knees, begging
for forgiveness.

But she had nothing to fear. King Alfred
was a just man. " Rise, good dame," he
said, " I betrayed your trust. You had
every reason to be angry. Go in peace."

This story may not be true, but at least
we know that Alfred was in Athelney,
because nine hundred years later, a gold
and enamel brooch belonging to him was
found in the marshes. On it were the words
" AElfred mee heht gewyrean." Which
means, in modern English " Alfred caused
me to be made."

While Alfred was in hiding in the marshes of Somerset, he set himself to gather together an army, and soon he had hundreds of men, armed and ready.

But before he attacked the Danes Alfred wanted to send a spy into their camp, to find out how many of them there were, and what sort of weapons they had. This was very dangerous, for if the Danes discovered the spy, they would kill him.

So Alfred decided to go himself. As well as being a brave fighter, Alfred could play on the harp and sing songs, and he boldly went into the Danes camp disguised as a minstrel.

The Danes liked music and singing and gladly welcomed him. So not only did Alfred find out all about them, but the leader of the Danes, Guthrum, paid him for his music.

Alfred now knew all that he needed to know about the Danish army, and he marched out of Athelney with his soldiers to meet the enemy.

The two armies met at Edington, in Wiltshire, and the English fought so fiercely that the Danes were completely defeated.

One reason for their defeat was that, early in the battle, the English captured the famous Raven banner. This was a flag with a great black bird embroidered on it, which the Danes believed had magic powers. Always it had brought them victory, and now that it was lost, the Danes lost heart also.

When these fierce fighting men saw that the banner had gone, they threw down their arms and surrendered.

With the defeat of Guthrum at Edington, Alfred had brought peace to England, at least for the time being. This was the first part of the task which he had set himself, so he now turned to the second.

Guthrum was a Dane and a heathen, and Alfred's life-long desire was to see England once more a Christian land. Guthrum and the heathens who followed him were now at Alfred's mercy, and one of the conditions of the terms of peace was that Guthrum and his men should become Christians.

They were all baptised in a great and impressive ceremony at a place near Athelney, and at this ceremony the heathen name of Guthrum was changed to Athelstan.

At the same time, Alfred and Athelstan agreed to divide England between them. Athelstan was to rule over all the land to the north of the Old Roman road called Watling Street, while Alfred was to remain King of the rest of England.

Many traces of this division of the country remain to this day, and the names of towns and villages ending in " -burgh " or " -by " or " -bury " show that the Danes built them. For example, Denby means the village of the Danes.

There are many other Danish words which we still use as names of places. Thorpe was the Danish word for a little town, and people still call the hills in the North of England by the Danish name of " fells."

For a long time the City of London had been in the hands of the Danes. That is why, you remember, Alfred had to be crowned at Winchester instead of in London. But now, by the arrangement with Athelstan, London again became part of Alfred's Kingdom.

When he entered London he found that it was mostly in ruins, and it was necessary to rebuild it almost completely.

Alfred, who was a very practical man, played a large part in this. He often went amongst the workmen, showing them how things should be done. Where the Romans had once built a fortress, Alfred raised a Saxon tower. This was afterwards rebuilt by William the Conqueror, and is the Tower of London which we know to-day.

For a while, England was peaceful. Athelstan kept his promise, and no longer marched with his men to attack the towns under Alfred.

But there were still a great many Danes over the seas, and these looked with envy on the rich and peaceful land of England. They were not bound by the treaty made with Athelstan and so once more, Danish ships appeared off the coast.

This time they were commanded by a Dane called Hastinga, after whom the English town of Hastings is named.

After attacking and burning towns on the coast, the Danes became bolder, and one morning they sailed right up the Thames to London, with eighty ships.

The news of enemy ships on the Thames was quickly brought to the King. But there was nothing he could do. At that time there was no British Navy, and Alfred had no ships of any kind which could fight the ships of Hastinga.

The Danes sailed on until they reached the River Lea, which joins the Thames about seven miles below London Bridge. Here they anchored their ships, and built a strong fort on the river bank.

The fort was too strong for Alfred and his men to attack, so he thought of another way of defeating the Danes. With all his men he started to build a dam across the river, and one morning the Danes awoke to find that their ships were high and dry.

When the Danes saw that their retreat by water was cut off, they lost heart. Leaving the fort which they had built on the river bank the Danes hurried away by land to the coast.

Soon they reached the other ships they had left there, and sailed away to their homeland in the North.

But Alfred had learned his lesson. He began to build ships, bigger and better ships than those of the Danes. Big oak trees were cut down in the royal forests, and in every harbour on the South Coast, shipwrights were busy.

This was the far-off beginning of what we to-day call the Royal Navy, whose ships have guarded our coasts ever since the days of Alfred.

From time to time the Danes did try to come back, but now they found that there were ships ready to fight them before they landed. Moreover, Alfred ordered men to keep watch on the cliffs all round the coast, so that whenever the enemy ships were sighted, the alarm was raised.

Immediately armed men lined the shore, and the English ships put out to sea. Soon the Danes realised that England, under the wise rule of King Alfred, was too strong for them.

For Alfred had not only built ships and arranged look-out posts on the cliffs: he had gathered all the men of England into an army called the " Fyrd." This was a sort of Home Guard, ready at any time to defend the homeland.

King Alfred had now achieved something which seemed impossible when he first came to the throne. He had brought peace to England, and united the whole country under his rule.

Now he could turn his thoughts to other things.

Ever since he had learned to read, as a little boy, Alfred had loved books. But there were no books written in a language which ordinary people in England could understand, so, in order to have time in which to write such books, Alfred decided that he would divide his day into three parts: eight hours working, eight hours sleeping, and eight hours of reading and writing new books in the English language.

But first Alfred had to have some way of telling the time, because clocks had not yet been invented, so he thought of the candle clock. This was a candle marked with coloured rings, one to each hour. As the candle burned down it showed how many hours had passed since it was lit.

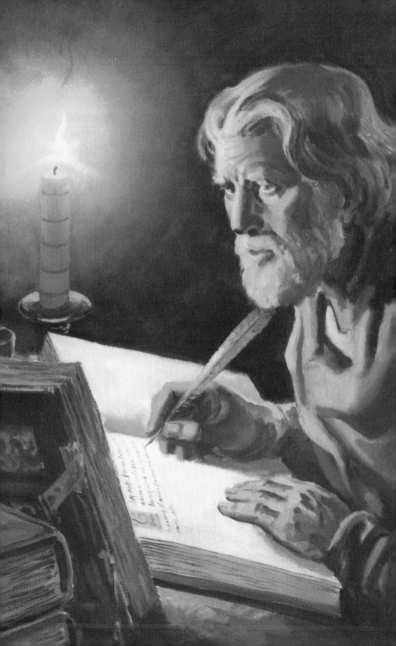

In King Alfred's time however, the ordinary people could not read. Only those who lived in monasteries were interested in reading and writing, or in learning anything except their own trade.

But without learning, and what is called research—that is, looking for new knowledge—there can be no progress.

Before the Danes came, there were many monasteries in England, but these had all been destroyed in the fighting up and down the country. Alfred therefore decided to build many new monasteries, and schools as well.

Scholars and teachers were brought to England from many countries, for Alfred knew what pleasure and knowledge he had himself gained from reading, and he wished all his people to learn to read and share his pleasure and ability to gain knowledge.

Part of Alfred's desire for knowledge was a wish to know more about other countries, and about those parts of the earth which had not yet been explored. So he encouraged men to go north and south, east and west, and then come back and tell him of the things they had seen.

One of these explorers was Othere, a very brave and tough sea captain.

Othere sailed away northward in his little ship, past the north of Scotland and the Orkney and Shetland Islands, and up the coast of Norway into the world of storms and ice. Here he found that in summer the sun never sets. This was something which no one from England had ever known or seen before, and Alfred wrote about this new knowledge which Othere had brought, in one of his books.

To-day, wherever you live in England, in town or country, you are in one of the shires into which Alfred divided his kingdom.

It was not easy for Alfred to do this in the days when there were no proper maps of the country, and no means of making them. So Alfred had to send men in all directions marking rivers, streams, hills and roads as the boundaries of counties and parishes.

That is why, to-day, these boundaries so often run along the banks of rivers; they have not changed since King Alfred's men passed that way, driving in posts to mark the divisions.

These were a few of the changes which the wise King Alfred achieved for England, and it is because of this that he is known in history as Alfred the Great.

But there is one other thing, perhaps the greatest of all, and the one which is most important to every one of us to-day.

English law and English justice are known and respected throughout the world, for in this country of ours it is almost impossible for an innocent man to be sent to prison. This we owe, in the first place, to King Alfred.

So England became a free country and we should always remember that it might have been very much less free if Alfred the Great had not lived and ruled, a thousand years ago.

MAP OF THE
SOUTH OF ENGLAND
Showing where the happenings
in this book took place

Line dividing Saxon

ENGLISH MERCIA

Here the Danes
surprised the
Saxons at
the Christmas
Feast

Chippenham

Ashdown
Here the Saxons cut a
White Horse on the downs

Edington

Capture of the
Raven Banner

Athelney
Alfred hiding
in the
marshes

WESSEX

Winchester
Alfred was crowned here